BipQuiz

100 QUESTIONS & ANSWERS

Great Inventions

BipQuiz

100 QUESTIONS & ANSWERS

Great Inventions

Illustrations by Bruno Heitz

Sterling Publishing Co., Inc.   New York

10 9 8 7 6 5 4 3 2 1
Published by Sterling Publishing Company, Inc.
387 Park Avenue South, New York, N.Y. 10016
© 1995 by Infomedia
English translation © 1995 by Sterling Publishing Co., Inc.
Distributed in Canada by Sterling Publishing
% Canadian Manda Group, One Atlantic Avenue, Suite 105
Toronto, Ontario, Canada M6K 3E7
Distributed in Great Britain and Europe by Cassell PLC
Wellington House, 125 Strand, London WC2R 0BB, England
Distributed in Australia by Capricorn Link (Australia) Pty Ltd.
P.O. Box 6651, Baulkham Hills, Business Centre, NSW 2153, Australia
Printed and bound in France
Sterling ISBN 0-8069-3828-5

How to Use the BipPen

The BipPen must be held straight to point to the black dot.

Point to a black dot.

●

A continuous sound (beeeep) and a red light mean that you've picked the wrong answer.

Point to a black dot.

●

A discontinuous sound (beep beep beep) and a green light mean that you've picked the right answer.

Keep your BipPen for other books.

Headings

Each question belongs to a specific heading.
Each heading is identified by a color.

Dates & Amounts

People & Places

Objects & Machines

Products & Materials

Methods

The wheel can be considered one of man's most useful inventions. The first wheels were used by:

potters ●

tinsmiths ■

blacksmiths ▲

Bread has been a dietary staple for thousands of years. The first breads contained no yeast, which is what makes the dough rise. These breads are called:

unleavened ●

manna ■

sourdough ▲

B efore the invention of the compass in the Middle Ages, the sun was used as a guide by day; by night man was guided by:

the moon ●
Polaris ■
Ursa Major ▲

O ne of the 20th century's chief inventions was that of the transistor in 1947 by J. Bardeen and W. Brattain. The transistor forms the basis of present-day electronics. In 1957, production was at:

10,000 units ●
1 million units ■
30 million units ▲

The aerosol spray can, in which a liquid or gas propels another material, was invented in 1926 by a Norwegian. But its marketing only began in 1941, when two Americans tried to sell:

perfume ●
deodorant ■
insecticide ▲

6

The perfection of the light bulb by Edison occurred in 1879. A bulb company was founded in 1883, and in two years it had sold:

1,000 light bulbs ●
10,000 light bulbs ■
80,000 light bulbs ▲

Anesthesia is a method of desensitizing a patient to pain. The first attempts to use it go all the way back to the 17th century; its practice became more generalized with the use of:

alcohol ●
brass knuckles ■
chloroform ▲

The Otis Elevator Company installed the first elevator in a New York department store. The use of the elevator led to the construction of skyscrapers. When was the elevator invented?

1857 ●
1930 ■
1950 ▲

The gasoline engine, invented by Daimler and perfected by Benz, was first put into vehicles in the 1880s. It is actually an improvement on another motor, the:

diesel engine ●

internal-combustion engine ■

four-stroke engine ▲

In 1908, the Model-T, one of the first assembly-line-made cars (up to 2000 a month in Detroit in 1909), emerged from the Ford factories. Before World War I this car cost:

$260 ●

$1200 ■

$5000 ▲

Griswold Lorillard, an American, invented the "smoking jacket," a man's evening outfit, inspired by what British men wore:

in the smoking room ●
when dining ■
to bed ▲

In 1783, the Montgolfier brothers were able to make a paper-and-fabric balloon rise to 5400 ft. Their first balloon rose thanks to:

hydrogen ●
helium ■
hot air ▲

I n 1644, E. Toricelli made the first mercury barometer that could measure atmospheric pressure. When the barometer rises, the weather will:

improve ●
worsen ■
stay the same ▲

B y using a principle similar to Archimedes' screw, an English farmer who built ship models patented the propeller, which replaced the previous means of ship propulsion, the:

flywheel ●
automatic oar ■
turbine ▲

The Romans were the first to use concrete (a mixture of pebbles, sand and cement) to build aqueducts. To make reinforced concrete, one must add:

tin
steel bars
gunpowder

The hammer, one of the oldest tools, was the first tool to have a handle. The steam sledgehammer, invented by Nasmyth in 1839, was first used in:

forges
planes
trains

C olors are obtained by mixing natural and (now) synthetic pigments with a binding agent. The ancient Egyptians got the color blue by crushing a semiprecious stone:

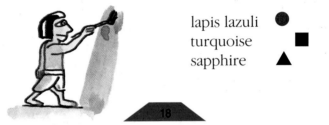

lapis lazuli ●
turquoise ■
sapphire ▲

T he internal-combustion engine works with an air–gas mixture that's lit by a flame, while in a diesel motor the gas is ignited by coming into contact with previously compressed hot air. This engine owes its name to:

Rudolf Diesel ●
Daisy Esel ■
the city of Essel ▲

As early as 2000 B.C., the Egyptians were using a sort of sundial to tell time. To know what time it was at night, they used a clepsydra, which is a:

water clock ●

priestess ■

flint watch ▲

The first machines for making nails were developed towards the end of the 18th century. But the oldest nails that have been found date back to:

3500 B.C. ●

the Roman Empire ■

the Middle Ages ▲

Candy maker Nicholas Appert invented a technique of food conservation in 1810, which consisted of heating foods in a closed container. The can was built by the British, and made of:

aluminum ●

tin ■

zinc ▲

The condom, which has been known since the Renaissance, only became widespread during the 19th century, thanks to the use of vulcanized rubber. The oral contraceptive pill was invented by an American in:

1712 ●

1956 ■

1983 ▲

In 1690, Denis Papin demonstrated the principle of the steam engine: A piston in a cylinder is moved by steam. This machine became the symbol of a revolution:

agricultural ●
industrial ■
cultural ▲

Liquid crystals are chemical products whose molecules change position when they're crossed by an electric current, creating zones of light. Such crystals are found in:

stained-glass windows ●
digital pictures ■
kaleidoscopes ▲

The first shock absorbers were placed in Egyptian Pharaoh Tutankhamen's chariot and were:

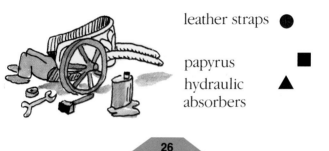

leather straps ●

papyrus ■

hydraulic absorbers ▲

The first artificial sparkling water (water + CO_2) was invented in 1741. Coca-Cola, invented by Pemberton, an American, in 1886, was considered:

alcohol ●
medication ■
candy ▲

In 1777 James Watt, a Scotsman, invented the first real steam engine. It was immediately used in a:

restaurant ●

mine shaft ■

museum ▲

After iron, aluminum is the most-often-used metal. Perfected in 1821, it was only used in industry towards the end of the 19th century. It comes from an ore called:

allumo ●

bauxite ■

minium ▲

The electrocardiogram was first used in 1903. It records the current produced by the activity and contractions of the:

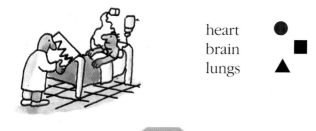

heart ●

brain ■

lungs ▲

The Sumerians were the first to use writing, around 3500 B.C. They impressed wedge-shaped characters on clay tablets, using sharpened reeds. What was this writing called?

cuneiform ●

pictographic ■

hieroglyphic ▲

31

Holland made one of the first submarines. One of its relatives was the:

car ●
ironclad ■
train ▲

32

Originally a mix of nitroglycerin and paper paste, dynamite was invented in 1867 by:

Dean A. Mite ●
the Nobel brothers ■
Paul Dynam ▲

Azipper is a system of hooks closed by a slide. It was invented in 1891, and was originally used for shoes, but was soon adapted to clothing. Before being perfected, its main drawback was that it:

stuck to the fabric ●
opened unexpectedly ■
rusted ▲

The first application of an optic fibre dates back to 1955. The principle of the fibre was discovered in:

1930 ●
1954 ■
1870 ▲

M oney first appeared in antiquity. Coins, which are much easier to use than barter, were first engraved with the likenesses of:

kings ●

gods ■

animals ▲

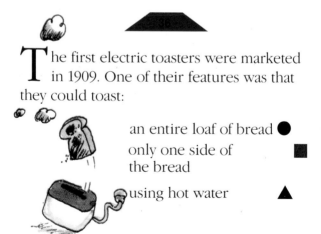

T he first electric toasters were marketed in 1909. One of their features was that they could toast:

an entire loaf of bread ●

only one side of the bread ■

using hot water ▲

The helicopter's ancestor flew in 1926. But a famous painter had drawn a flying machine that very much resembled a helicopter during the 16th century. Who was he?

Raphael ●

Michelangelo ■

Leonardo da Vinci ▲

The lie detector, invented in 1921, measures blood pressure, cardiac rhythm, and sweating. This last parameter is measured by:

water weight ●

skin's resistance to
electrical currents ■

dilation of the skin's
pores ▲

The Babylonians invented the 24-hour day and the 60-minute hour in about 3000 B.C. Time is now measured by the vibrations of a crystal:

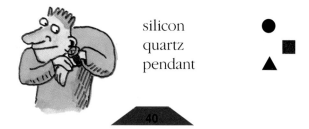

silicon ●

quartz ■

pendant ▲

On December 17, 1903, the Wright brothers made their historic airplane flight on the dunes of Kitty Hawk. Which state is it in?

North Dakota ●

North Carolina ■

South Carolina ▲

The atomic bomb was developed in the 1940s. Where was it first exploded?

New York   ●
New Mexico   ■
Denver   ▲

The first credit card to be used for daily purchases was issued in 1950. Americans had been using credit cards since 1920 for the purchase of:

housewares   ●

gas   ■

furniture   ▲

I n the 12th century, in European royal courts, the fork assumed its present shape. But its ancestor was being used as early as the 11th century in Italy to eat:

fruit

oysters

potatoes

C larence Birdseye produced the first frozen foods in 1924. Another form of conservation consists of drying foods at low temperature and in a vacuum. This process is called:

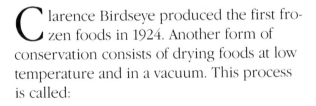

freeze-drying

dehydration

disintegration

Ball bearings allow for movement without wearing out the materials that contain them. The bearings were patented for use on:

bicycles
planes
trains

The German printer Gutenberg invented a mould to cast metal letters. Which famous work of his appeared in 1453?

a grammar
an encyclopedia
a Bible

Television was on display at New York's World Fair in 1938, and was in mass production by the late 1940s. Who was one of the first stars of the small screen?

Milton Berle ●

Jack Kerouac ■

Jerry Lewis ▲

Invented in the U.S., blue jeans are made with a very strong fabric. These pants were incredibly successful among cowboys and:

gold miners ●

Indians ■

soldiers ▲

The first jukebox was installed in a San Francisco saloon. This machine's name comes from the slang word *jukehouse*, which means:

sanctuary ●

chapel ■

wicked house ▲

The laser is a ray of light that's uniform in color and perfectly straight. Its inventor, Townes, won the Nobel prize in 1964. The laser is used in surgery as a:

scalpel ●

compress ■

light ▲

During the Middle Ages, Roger Bacon, an Englishman, was the first to think of using convex lenses and contact lenses to correct farsightedness. Concave lenses are used to correct nearsightedness, also called:

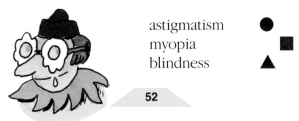

astigmatism ●

myopia ■

blindness ▲

An American mechanic, Singer, patented the first sewing machine in 1851. The first needle dates back to the:

Stone Age ●

Middle Ages ■

Renaissance ▲

The arms manufacturer Remington put a new kind of machine on the market in 1874:

washing machine ●

typewriter ■

calculator ▲

The use of postage stamps began in England in 1840. The first stamp pictured Queen Victoria. Before that, postage had been paid by the:

addressee ●

carrier ■

sender ▲

The first patent for a motorcycle dates back to 1868. In 1914, the speed record for a motorcycle was:

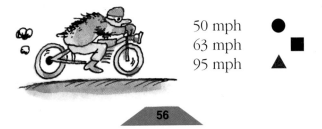

50 mph ●
63 mph ■
95 mph ▲

Although Faraday was able to demonstrate the capabilities of the electric motor in 1821, he was unable to build one. In 1835, Davenport, an American, did build one. He was a:

blacksmith ●
mechanic ■
pharmacist ▲

Thomas Edison perfected the movie camera. He had two laboratories in New Jersey, the first in Menlo Park and the second in:

West Milford   ●
West Orange   ■
East Orange   ▲

A patent is filed to protect the inventor and allow him to develop and propagate his idea. The inventor may give his distribution rights on his patent to someone else by giving the distributor:

a license   ●
a receipt   ■
an expertise   ▲

The spirit level, a small wooden ruler with a little glass tube filled with a liquid and an air bubble, has been known since the Middle Ages. The level is used to find the horizontal and vertical planes. The tube contains:

water
alcohol
oil

The first pair of roller skates appeared in London in 1760. A Belgian lute maker invented them to demonstrate during a:

masked ball
contest
exam

The first computer, built in the U.S. in 1945, had 18,000 electronic tubes ("ancestors" of our present-day chips) and used perforated cards. The machine weighed:

650 lbs. ●
1 ton ■
30 tons ▲

Paper was made by the Chinese during the 2nd century B.C. It was brought into Europe during the Middle Ages by the Arabs, when they invaded Spain. The Egyptians wrote on:

cotton ●
lotus ■
papyrus ▲

Carbon paper was invented in 1806. When put between two sheets of paper, it copies the text written on the first sheet onto the second. Carbonless copies are done by:

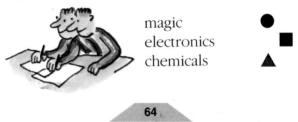

magic ●

electronics ■

chemicals ▲

Pasteurization, named for Louis Pasteur, consists of heating foods at temperatures between 140° and 184°F for a few instants to:

change the taste ●

kill bacteria ■

change the texture ▲

The Alexandria lighthouse, in Egypt, was 350 ft. tall and topped with a beacon visible from a distance of over 30 miles. It constituted one of the:

7 wonders of the world ●
12 tasks of Hercules ■
10 plagues of Egypt ▲

The velocipede, an ancestor of the bicycle, was built in 1839 by Mac Millan, a British blacksmith. It was the first machine to be propelled by pedals, and was made of:

iron ●
steel ■
wood ▲

Celluloid was perfected in 1869 by mixing cellulose nitrate and camphor. It was dangerous because it was flammable. It was replaced by synthetic products, although it is still used for:

golf balls ●
Ping-Pong balls ■
tennis balls ▲

Americans searched for an artificial fibre to compete with imported Japanese silk. Such a fibre was invented by W. Carothers and was called:

linen ●
polyester ■
nylon ▲

T he fountain pen was first commercialized in the U.S. by L. E. Waterman. The disposable ink cartridge was invented in:

1900 ●
1930 ■
1950 ▲

I n the 1970s the microchip revolutionized the electronics industry. Many chip companies were founded in which area of California?

Silicon Valley ●
Napa Valley ■
Coachella Valley ▲

As early as 1922, Marconi had thought of using radio waves to detect the presence of ships in the fog. It was only in 1931 that the first radar device was built. In 1936, an instrument like radar was placed on a ship to detect:

planes
icebergs
submarines

The first pencil was invented in 1795. The ballpoint pen appeared in the:

1960s
1900s
1930s

I n 1897, W. Cannon, while still a student at Harvard, showed that one could photograph the intestines of a dog that had drunk a bismuth solution, thanks to:

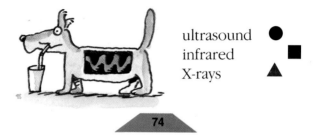

ultrasound ●

infrared ■

X-rays ▲

A mpex made the fist videotape recorder in 1956. The first videocassette was sold in 1969 by:

Philips ●

Sony ■

RCA ▲

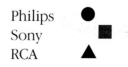

E dison had over 1000 patents, including those for the electric light bulb and the phonograph. On the day of his burial, he was honored throughout the U.S. by:

electric lights were
lowered for a minute ●

phonographs being turned on ■

banks closing ▲

T he first photograph was taken by Niepce in 1827. With his "black box," he focused the view from his window onto a tin plate. The exposure lasted:

10 minutes ●

30 hours ■

8 hours ▲

G alileo made an astronomical telescope in 1609. He used it to observe other planets and he suggested that the earth:

circles the sun ●
wobbles ■
is a satellite of the ▲
moon

S ynthetic aspirin was first perfected by the German chemist Felix Hoffman in 1897. Aspirin was first extracted from the bark of the:

plane tree ●
willow ■
birch ▲

An American in 1845 patented the design of the light bulb: a carbon filament brought to incandescence by the passage of an electric current in a bulb in which there is:

a vacuum
some water
some hydrogen

Braille, the raised alphabet used by the blind, bears the name of its inventor, Louis Braille. Blinded at 3, he conceived of his alphabet at the age of:

15
30
50

A synthetic resin, which was both excellent for insulation and easy to mould, was invented in 1908. It influenced the design of objects until the 1950s. What is it?

polonium ●
Bakelite ■
manganese ▲

Originally, railroads were used solely to transport coal in mines, and railroad cars were still pulled by horses. The first steam locomotive appeared in 1803, in:

Germany ●
England ■
France ▲

T he first escalator, put into service in 1894, is actually an inclined moving rug. The number of people transported by escalators each year in the world is thought to be:

100 million ●
500 million ■
over 50 billion ▲

S ewers, in use before 2500 B.C., were constructed during antiquity, mainly by the:

Gauls ●
Romans ■
Greeks ▲

The simple gears known since antiquity are composed of two toothed wheels whose teeth mesh with each other, making them turn. A differing number of teeth implies:

different speeds ●
different movements ■
different materials ▲

In 1752, Benjamin Franklin invented the lightning rod, which could channel the electric discharge of lightning bolts into the ground. Franklin was also a:

doctor ●
seismologist ■
statesman ▲

The first traces of irrigation, used by the Egyptians, date back to 5000 B.C. Archimedes' screw (from 250 B.C.) was used to:

close canals ●
lift oxen ■
raise water from the ▲
    Nile

The phonograph, invented by Thomas Edison, reproduces recorded sounds. Compact digital disks are now read by a:

diamond ●
laser ■
microgroove ▲

The first newspaper dates back about 1000 years, and was distributed in the imperial Chinese court on handwritten sheets. Its propagation accelerated during the 15th century, thanks to the:

printing press ●
transcribers ■
ballpoint pens ▲

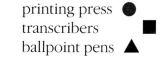

It's possible to see the inside of the human body thanks to the CAT scan, invented in 1973. A detector measures variations in the density of tissue through which an X-ray passes. This device was originally solely used to explore the:

heart ●
blood ■
brain ▲

The first radio transmission of a human voice dates back to 1906, and was made possible by the work of:

Radioni ●
Marconi ■
Volta ▲

The life jacket was first made, in 1854, of pieces of cork sewn into a fabric belt. Where did this invention come from?

Belgium ●
England ■
an unknown source ▲

Alexander Graham Bell perfected the telephone: sound waves were transformed into electrical current which was then transmitted by a cable to a receiver that reconstituted the voice. Bell's patent predated a similar one only by a few:

days ●
hours ■
months ▲

T he first beer brewers, the Mesopotamians, invented beer between 8000 and 6000 B.C. They mixed warm water with a cereal that germinated and fermented. Which cereal was it?

rye
hops
rice

G lass, which was in use 5000 years ago, was a costly and rare material. During the Middle Ages, it was used for stained glass and was only mass-produced during the 19th century. It is prepared from:

mother of pearl
sand
salt

The first underground subway was built in 1863 in:

London ●
New York ■
Paris ▲

In 1970, a laser device was perfected to listen to conversations by pointing the laser through a window. For the device to be effective, the windows had to be:

clean ●
open ■
dirty ▲

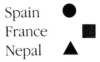

The cable car dates back to the 15th century. The first one built for travellers was installed in 1911 in:

Spain ●
France ■
Nepal ▲

The telegraph, which allows for the sending of coded messages in the form of dots and dashes at the rate of ten words per minute, was invented in 1837, and is named after its inventor:

Morse ●
Codex ■
Braille ▲

The first submarine was built around 1620 by Drebbel, a Dutchman. Used from the beginning for military purposes, it sank its first victim during:

the Civil War ●
WWI ■
WWII ▲

The Invention of Writing

The first writing, composed of pictograms that represented objects or actions, was invented in Mesopotamia around 3500 B.C. This invention was made necessary by the evolution of Mesopotamian society. The beginnings of commerce among cities made it necessary to inventory and account for merchandise. Writing began to evolve rapidly towards more ab-

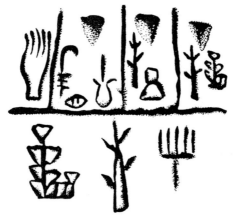

The first pictograms were invented by the Sumerians.

stract forms: Drawings became simplified and were reduced to signs. Pictograms gave way to ideograms, whose meanings were more symbolic. Finally, certain forms of writing evolved in such a manner that the signs no longer had anything to do with the meaning of the words. Alphabets allowed for the formation of an infinite number of words.

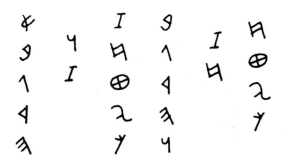

The Phoenicians invented the first alphabet, later perfected by the Greeks.

Hieroglyphs were ideograms representing objects and ideas.